Sans Peur: A Small Book of Poetry

S.J. Sutherland

Sans Peur: A Small Book of Poetry © 2022
S.J. Sutherland

All rights reserved.

No part of this publication may be reproduced, stored in a retrieval system, or transmitted, in any form or by any means, electronic, mechanical, photocopying, recording or otherwise, without the prior written permission of the presenters.

S.J. Sutherland asserts the moral right to be identified as author of this work.

Presentation by *BookLeaf Publishing*

Web: www.bookleafpub.com

E-mail: info@bookleafpub.com

ISBN: 978-93-95755-63-4

First edition 2022

For H.B.

My first audience and friend.

ACKNOWLEDGEMENT

Moments of great joy and sorrow - as well as quiet, reflective days and nights - inspired the writings contained herein. I'm thankful to my God for the gift that was every moment.

PREFACE

This little book is equal parts passion project and therapeutic outlet, spanning snapshots from my life in no particular order over the past year or so. To all readers, I humbly ask that you take inspiration from this book's title and venture forth with me on paths not tread, without fear.

Cloud nine.

Today I floated up to cloud nine
Sunburnt, full and happy
I passed clouds one through eight on my way
And felt a little sad
Aren't the others lonely?

Falling (Behind)

Catch up, catch up
The winds whispered to me
As they played with my hair and softly kissed my cheek
An empty promise of more to come
Yet the faster I moved, the farther my target moved from me
A game I had not agreed to play
And now I was losing, badly
The mountain and the sea met at eye level
And wished me luck as I fell (behind)

Seagull on the car roof

He landed on the car rooftop
Swooping in low and fast
He held a spot where I felt at home
Then soared again, with me

(Trans)planted.

I've sat in my pot for years,
Safe, sheltered, happy, mostly well-fed
Why is this haven now hurting me?

My soil is dark, cool, life-giving,
Like a gentle rainfall on dry land
I come up to the surface, gasping for breath
Afraid to branch out on my own, yet

Unable to keep still and silent any more
I soak in the air and sun - a sponge about to
burst - and feel the beginning of something new

I started so small, yet now I
Overshadow even my own expectations
It seems I have outgrown myself

The unknown is so scary though, so I sit back,
waiting, not noticing at first that I am getting
sick

As pieces of me start to droop, then fall,
The need for change is inescapable

How do I make a new home, home?

Will my roots survive the transplanting?
Yet I must return to green, so I move
Forward, onward, desperate - a coachman
driving his team through a storm

Home (and health) awaits

Airport Cemetery

A silent chorus watched us join the clouds today
Did they cheer us as we 'parted?
Or did they curse the interruption to their slumber
The thousandth roar overhead?

Sleep on, dear dreamers
We will all join you at our own appointed time
Some flights cannot be missed

Indoor Thunderstorm

Tonight a storm erupted in my living room
The winds blew, lightning flashed and thunder crashed
Yet all my cushions are dry
The carpet clean
How can I measure the millimeters of rain inside (me)?

33900

Was the number of kilometres my car hit that night
Driving home from your house
That night I felt my lip quiver as
Thoughts came rolling back over me
An ocean of memories
Some warm and contenting
Others icy and numb
Why did I dive back in to this current?
My desperate attempts to cling on to you
Are like clinging to a piece of driftwood in a flash flood
Why did I think I could outrun, outsmart, outpace, outcry myself?
My streak is evaporating, I'm left with only out.

02.13.4:25

A pregnant pause,
A moment to weigh, decide the outcome
A leaning in, closing the distance
So distinct, yet so familiar
Words not said, yet we both know
A gentle sigh as hands caress
We fell into each other
But landed oh so softly
His mouth was strange yet home.

Chipped Nail

On the last day of age 29
Quietly and without cause
I chipped the end off one of my nails
My goal of reaching 30 whole now spoiled

Is it a sign to leave behind pieces of my 20s
Broken yet still beautiful
In the present soon to be past?

I'm encouraged to remember
Much like my nails can be reshaped and grow back stronger
So can I
My 30s hold so much

Floating cities

Floating cities
Made of white
Who can tell your splendour?

You drift apart from day to day
Indifferent to your might

Is this where Heaven makes it home?
Indwelling, hidden, glorious
I long to rest amongst the clouds
But they break apart, too fragile

Thief.

Comparison is the thief of joy
And she needs to be locked up for grand larceny
I don't want her company anymore
She's taken too much
From me

Jealousy moved in as her roommate
And owes months of back rent
How do you shake down an idea?

I want to steal away
Into the night
And not look back
NYC, Boston, Chicago… here I come

Time Travel

As I sat in an airplane
Fighting off the need to sleep
I woke up with a start and realized
How much time had yet had not passed
4 years past gently collided with the present
The hum and roar of silence surrounded around me
As my eyes fluttered back to sleep
My younger self smiled in the darkness
And jostled me with her elbow

Family Drive

Here we go
Clouds and language swirling
Moving from one home to another
I seek and cannot wait to find
As we head out on a family drive…

Shift

I feel a shift in my heart and mind tonight
Something almost uncomfortable
Like you've forgotten to check if the stove is off
But have headed out for the night

I wish I could say-
I love you.

Bare Thoughts

Your scent is all around me
What do I do with myself?
I now know better why one half of the closet
Stays fully stocked long after expiration
Anything to stay closer to you
The empty arms draw me in close
Again

Ripped from Sleep

The most violent of passive crimes
Limbs tingling, all aglow
My body burns while numb
Ripped from sleep's dark rhythmic flow

Ripped from sleep
It's torn to pieces
Scared, my heartbeat racing fast
A spring uncoiled, frozen, nascent
Then galloping much faster back

Someone say there is no danger
Someone share the fear has passed

Poem about Love

Love is a glass of water when you are thirsty
On the hottest day of the year
The air conditioner broken by the kids down the hall
The mechanic can't come until tomorrow and
Meanwhile your tongue goes dry
Ice cannot quench this thirst
A bead of sweat travels down your back
After an hour your body slows down
Preserve preserve preserve
It wills itself
Then, sweat sticking to my shirt, you hand me a glass of water
And I felt the love and condensation drip down my hand.

Do

One thing I love about you
Is that you do
Not going to
But do

Thank you.

CPSIA information can be obtained
at www.ICGtesting.com
Printed in the USA
BVHW051159270623
666442BV00016B/1092